Hark, hark, the lark at Heaven's gate sings!

WILLIAM SHAKESPEARE

*Spring flowers are in blossom all over.*
*The whole world's a choir—and singing!*
THE MESSAGE

LITERARY PORTALS TO PRAYER™

# WILLIAM SHAKESPEARE

ILLUMINATED BY

COMPILED AND INTRODUCED BY

RON MARASCO

WILLIAM SHAKESPEARE
Illuminated by The Message
Compiled and introduced by Ron Marasco

Series Editor, Gregory F. Augustine Pierce

Design and typesetting by Harvest Graphics

Cover image by Bigstock, © Tony Baggett

Published by ACTA Publications, 4848 N. Clark St.,
Chicago, IL 60640, (800) 397-2282, actapublications.com

Copyright © 2015 by Ron Marasco

Scripture taken from *The Message: Catholic/Ecumenical Edition* Copyright © 2013 by
Eugene H. Petersen all rights reserved. Licensed with permission of NavPress. Represented
by Tyndale House Publishers Inc. Carol Stream, Illinois 60188.

*The Message* and *The Message* logo are registered trademarks of NavPress. Used by
permission. All rights reserved.

Library of Congress Number: 2015948536
ISBN: 978-0-87946-621-3 (standard edition)
ISBN: 978-0-87946-627-5 (enhanced-size edition)
Printed in the United States of America by Total Printing Systems
Year 20 19 18 17 16 15
Printing 12 11 10 9 8 7 6 5 4 3 2 First

♻ Text printed on 30% post-consumer recycled paper

# CONTENTS

# A NOTE FROM THE PUBLISHER / 9

# HIS FATHER'S HOUSE / 11

# PORTALS TO PRAYER / 15

Prayer is sometimes difficult. Perhaps we need spiritual inspiration. Something to reignite our spiritual life. A way to initiate a new and fruitful spiritual direction.

Great literature can do these things: inspire, ignite, and initiate.

Which is why ACTA Publications is publishing a series of "Literary Portals to Prayer." The idea is simple: Take insightful passages from great authors whose work has stood the test of time and illuminate each selection with a well-chosen quotation from the Bible on the same theme.

To do this, we use a relatively new translation by Eugene Peterson called *The Message: Catholic/Ecumenical Edition*. It is a fresh, compelling, challenging, and faith-filled translation of the Scriptures from ancient languages into contemporary American English that sounds as if it was written yesterday. *The Message* may be new to you, or you may already know it well, but see if it doesn't illuminate these writings of William Shakespeare in delightful ways.

We publish the books in this series in a size that can easily fit in pocket or purse and find a spot on kitchen table, bed stand, work bench, study desk, or exercise machine. We also publish each title in an enhanced size for both public and private use. These books are meant to be used in a variety of ways. And we feature a variety of authors so you can find the one or ones that can kick-start your prayer life.

So enjoy these portals to prayer by William Shakespeare

illuminated by *The Message*. And look for others in this series, including Louisa May Alcott, Hans Christian Andersen, Jane Austen, Charles Dickens, Elizabeth Gaskell, Herman Melville, and others. Consider them, if you will, literary lectio divina.

Gregory F. Augustine Pierce
President and Publisher
ACTA Publications

William Shakespeare lived in a time when being a person-of-faith was not only difficult, it was dangerous. As one "official" religion fell out of favor with the State and was replaced by another, those caught practicing the "wrong" faith were subject to persecution and even death. Though fear was pervasive, it could not sever every individual's connection to their personal spirituality. Instead, some people's faith found expression in other forms. In the case of William Shakespeare, I believe, religion's loss was Renaissance literature's gain, and hidden beneath a surface of what seem to be purely "secular" plays and poetry is a depth of soul that literary-critics have long called "genius" but that people of faith would recognize as prayer.

We have no indisputable proof that Shakespeare was a professed member of any religion. The man who once wrote "In peace there's nothing so becomes a man as modest stillness and humility," led, indeed, a peaceful life and was, by all accounts, a gentle, humble guy. I think he was too self-effacing a writer to ever tip his hand about his own faith. That said, there is one key person in his life that many scholars believe *was* a Catholic. And it is someone I believe Shakespeare loved very much: his father, John.

The husband of Mary Shakespeare and father of William made his living in Stratford-upon-Avon as a glover—a tough occupation (more akin to being a butcher in a slaughterhouse than a proprietor of a *Louis Vuitton* boutique). John Shakespeare was the town ale-taster, a part-time constable, and a street-wise man who—being illiterate—signed documents with his mark, the shaky sketch of a metal "compass," a tool used by glovers to score leather.

Though his son would go on to chronicle the lives great men, John Shakespeare was not a great man. He was a failure at business, often debt-ridden and, at times, in minor scrapes with the law. But he was a good soul, and a warm father, and known throughout his town as a "merry-cheeked old man" who once said of his son, Will, that they liked "to jest" with each other. And, since a parent with a good sense of humor is every actor's first audience, Shakespeare loved him. You can see this affection in some characters in his plays. His father is there in all those rough-hewn, loveably-flawed tavern-philosophers and enchanting rouges, like Falstaff or Nick Bottom or the red-nosed Bardolph or Constable Dogberry.

In the eighteenth century, long generations after William Shakespeare was buried in the chancery of Holy Trinity Church in Stratford, a bricklayer working on a house once owned by John Shakespeare discovered an old document, tucked away in the rafters behind a wall. It was a spiritual testament, a personal Profession of Faith that Catholics living in those perilous Elizabethan times would share, in secret, with their like-minded faithful. For years, this extraordinary find was deemed "a fake" by skeptical scholars. (Is there any other kind of scholar?!) But faith, as they also say of *truth*, "will out." And, in the twentieth century, scholars discovered the source of the text found in the wall of John Shakespeare's house.

The precise wording came from the Italian Cardinal, Carlo Borromeo, who historians have connected to Fr. Edmund

Campion, the famous Jesuit priest and martyr who lived in Shakespeare's time—and who was known to have preached Catholicism in the region where John Shakespeare lived. Since it would not have been possible for some enterprising eighteenth-century bricklayer—even in cahoots with a clever forger—to fake the exact wording of a spiritual testament that lay undiscovered till centuries later, scholars believe the Stratford document to be true and, thus, that John Shakespeare was Catholic. For me, the clincher is the name given to the last of John and Mary Shakespeare's children, a boy born one year before Campion was martyred, whom they christened "Edmund."

At the time of Edmund Shakespeare's birth in Stratford (1580) and Edmund Campion's notorious martyrdom at Tyburn in London (1581), William Shakespeare was around sixteen years old. I cannot imagine such a perceptive mind, at such an impressionable age, did not sense some of the feelings that may have been going on in the conflicted soul of his father.

If John Shakespeare was a man of faith, he was not a brave one; and, whatever he felt about God in his heart, he kept the "proof" of his religion hidden behind a wall. But, for all of his flaws, he raised a son who loved him, and who learned from his Catholic dad. A son who heard the prayers his father dared not speak and found a way to say them *for* him, writing them into his plays and hiding them in the rafters of his poetry for us to find.

Ron Marasco
Loyola Marymount University
Los Angeles, California

WILLIAM SHAKESPEARE

SELECTIONS FROM

*As You Like It*
*Cymbeline*
*Epitaph, Anne Hathaway's Grave*
*Epitaph, William Shakespeare's Grave*
*Hamlet*
*Henry the Fifth*
*Henry the Sixth, Part Two*
*Henry the Sixth, Part Three*
*Henry the Eighth*
*Julius Caesar*
*King John*
*King Lear*
*Macbeth*
*Measure for Measure*
*The Merchant of Venice*
*A Midsummer Night's Dream*
*The Phoenix and Turtle*
*Richard the Second*
*Romeo and Juliet*
*Sir Thomas More*
*The Sonnets*
*The Tempest*
*Twelfth Night*
*Venus and Adonis*

### A PLACE OF SAFETY

God shall be my hope,
My stay, my guide, and lantern to my feet;
And go in peace....

HENRY THE SIXTH, PART TWO, II. iii. 24-26

### A PLACE OF SAFETY

*I run to you, GOD; I run for dear life.*
    *Don't let me down!*
    *Take me seriously this time!*
*Get down on my level and listen,*
    *and please—no procrastination!*
*Your granite cave a hiding place,*
    *your high cliff aerie a place of safety.*

*You're my cave to hide in,*
    *my cliff to climb.*
*Be my safe leader,*
    *be my true mountain guide.*
*Free me from hidden traps;*
    *I want to hide in you.*
*I've put my life in your hands.*
    *You won't drop me,*
    *you'll never let me down.*

PSALM 31:1-5

### ALL THESE MIRACLE-WONDERS

Who will believe my verse in time to come
If it were filled with your most high deserts?
Though yet Heaven knows it is but as a tomb
Which hides your life, and shows not half your parts.
If I could write the beauty of Your eyes,
And in fresh numbers number all Your graces,
The age to come would say, "This poet lies,
Such Heavenly touches ne'er touched earthly faces."

SONNET 17, 1-8

## ALL THESE MIRACLE-WONDERS

*"Are you listening? Have you noticed all this?*
*Stop in your tracks!*
*Take in God's miracle-wonders!*
*Do you have any idea how God does it all,*
*how he makes bright lightning from dark storms,*
*How he piles up the cumulus clouds—*
*all these miracle-wonders of a perfect Mind?*
*Why, you don't even know how to keep cool*
*on a sweltering hot day,*
*So how could you even dream*
*of making a dent in that hot-tin-roof sky?*

JOB 37:14-18

## MAKE YOURSELF AT HOME IN LOVE

Here the anthem doth commence:
Love and Constancy is dead,
Phoenix and the Turtle fled
In a mutual flame from hence.

So they loved as love in twain
Had the essence but in one,
Two distincts, division none;
Number there in love was slain.

Hearts remote, yet not asunder;
Distance and no space was seen
'Twixt this Turtle and his queen:
But in them it were a wonder.

So between them love did shine,
That the Turtle saw his right
Flaming in the Phoenix' sight;
Either was the other's mine.

THE PHOENIX AND TURTLE, 21-36

### MAKE YOURSELF AT HOME IN LOVE

"I've loved you the way my Father has loved me. Make yourselves at home in my love. If you keep my commands, you'll remain intimately at home in my love. That's what I've done—kept my Father's commands and made myself at home in his love.

"I've told you these things for a purpose: that my joy might be your joy, and your joy wholly mature. This is my command: Love one another the way I loved you. This is the very best way to love. Put your life on the line for your friends. You are my friends when you do the things I command you. I'm no longer calling you servants because servants don't understand what their master is thinking and planning. No, I've named you friends because I've let you in on everything I've heard from the Father.

"You didn't choose me, remember; I chose you, and put you in the world to bear fruit, fruit that won't spoil. As fruit bearers, whatever you ask the Father in relation to me, he gives you.

"But remember the root command: Love one another."

JOHN 15:9-17

21

### THE TOOLS OF OUR TRADE

The poet's eye, in a fine frenzy rolling,
Doth glance from Heaven to earth,
From earth to Heaven;
And as imagination bodies forth
The form of things unknown, the poet's pen
Turns them to shapes, and gives to airy nothing
A local habitation and a name.
Such tricks hath strong imagination,
That if it would but apprehend some joy,
It comprehends some bringer of that joy;
Or in the night, imagining some fear,
How easy is a bush supposed a bear!

A MIDSUMMER NIGHT'S DREAM, V. i. 11-22

### THE TOOLS OF OUR TRADE

*The world is unprincipled. It's dog-eat-dog out there! The world doesn't fight fair. But we don't live or fight our battles that way—never have and never will. The tools of our trade aren't for marketing or manipulation, but they are for demolishing that entire massively corrupt culture. We use our powerful God-tools for smashing warped philosophies, tearing down barriers erected against the truth of God, fitting every loose thought and emotion and impulse into the structure of life shaped by Christ. Our tools are ready at hand for clearing the ground of every obstruction and building lives of obedience into maturity.*

2 CORINTHIANS 10:3-6

### TOIL AND TROUBLE

What a piece of work is a man, how noble in reason, how infinite in faculties, in form and moving, how express and admirable, in action how like an angel, in apprehension how like a god! The beauty of the world, the paragon of animals! And yet, to me, what is this quintessence of dust?

HAMLET, II. ii. 303-308

### TOIL AND TROUBLE

*So don't return us to mud, saying,*
  *"Back to where you came from!"*
*Patience! You've got all the time in the world—whether*
  *a thousand years or a day, it's all the same to you.*
*Are we no more to you than a wispy dream,*
  *no more than a blade of grass*
*That springs up gloriously with the rising sun*
  *and is cut down without a second thought?*
*Your anger is far and away too much for us;*
  *we're at the end of our rope.*
*You keep track of all our sins; every misdeed*
  *since we were children is entered in your books.*
*All we can remember is that frown on your face.*
  *Is that all we're ever going to get?*
*We live for seventy years or so*
  *(with luck we might make it to eighty),*
*And what do we have to show for it? Trouble.*
  *Toil and trouble and a marker in the graveyard.*
*Who can make sense of such rage,*
  *such anger against the very ones who fear you?*

PSALM 90:3-11

25

### READY TO SEE AND HEAR AND ACT

How sweet the moonlight sleeps upon this bank!
Here will we sit, and let the sounds of music
Creep in our ears. Soft stillness and the night
Become the touches of sweet harmony....
Look how the floor of Heaven
Is thick inlaid with patens of gold.
There's not the smallest orb which thou behold'st
But in this motion like an angel sings,
Still choiring to the young-eyed cherubins;
Such harmony is in immortal souls,
But while this muddy vesture of decay
Doth grossly close it in, we cannot hear it.

**THE MERCHANT OF VENICE, V. i. 54-65**

## READY TO SEE AND HEAR AND ACT

*Not everybody is ready for this, ready to see and hear and act. Isaiah asked what we all ask at one time or another: "Does anyone care, God? Is anyone listening and believing a word of it?" The point is: Before you trust, you have to listen.*

ROMANS 10:16-17

### STEEP YOURSELF

Be not afeared, the isle is of full of noises,
Sounds, and sweet airs, that give delight and hurt not.
Sometimes a thousand twangling instruments
Will hum about mine ears; and sometime voices,
That if I then had waked after long sleep,
Will make me sleep again; and then in dreaming,
The clouds methought would open, and show riches
Ready to drop upon me, that when I waked
I cried to dream again.

THE TEMPEST, III. ii. 135-143

### STEEP YOURSELF

"What I'm trying to do here is get you to relax, not be so preoccupied with getting so you can respond to God's giving. People who don't know God and the way he works fuss over these things, but you know both God and how he works. Steep yourself in God-reality, God-initiative, God-provisions. You'll find all your everyday human concerns will be met. Don't be afraid of missing out. You're my dearest friends! The Father wants to give you the very kingdom itself."

LUKE 12:29-32

### THIS VISION-MESSAGE

I have had a most rare vision. I have had a dream, past the wit of man to say what dream it was.... Man is but a patched fool if he will offer to say what methought I had. The eye of man hath not heard, the ear of man hath not seen, man's hand is not able to taste, his tongue to conceive, nor his heart to report, what my dream was. I will get Peter Quince to write a ballad of this dream. It shall be called "Bottom's Dream," because it hath no bottom.

A MIDSUMMER NIGHT'S DREAM,
IV. i. 204-206, 209-216

### THIS VISION-MESSAGE

*And then God answered: "Write this.*
    *Write what you see.*
*Write it out in big block letters*
    *so that it can be read on the run.*
*This vision-message is a witness*
    *pointing to what's coming.*
*It aches for the coming—it can hardly wait!*
    *And it doesn't lie.*
*If it seems slow in coming, wait.*
    *It's on its way. It will come right on time.*

HABAKKUK 2:2-3

### LOVE NEVER GIVES UP

O spirit of love, how quick and fresh art thou,
That, notwithstanding thy capacity,
Receiveth as the sea, nought enters there,
Of what validity and pitch so e'er,
But falls in to abatement and low price
Even in a minute! So full of shapes is fancy
That it alone is high fantastical.

TWELFTH NIGHT, I. i. 9-15

### LOVE NEVER GIVES UP

*Love never gives up.*
*Love cares more for others than for self.*
*Love doesn't want what it doesn't have.*
*Love doesn't strut,*
*Doesn't have a swelled head,*
*Doesn't force itself on others,*
*Isn't always "me first,"*
*Doesn't fly off the handle,*
*Doesn't keep score of the sins of others,*
*Doesn't revel when others grovel,*
*Takes pleasure in the flowering of truth,*
*Puts up with anything,*
*Trusts God always,*
*Always looks for the best,*
*Never looks back,*
*But keeps going to the end.*

I CORINTHIANS 13:4-7

### WORTHY OF RESPECT

Lord of my love, to whom in vassalage
Thy merit hath my duty strongly knit,
To thee I send this written ambassage,
To witness duty, not to show my wit;
Duty so great, which wit so poor as mine
May make seem bare, in wanting words to show it,
But that I hope some good conceit of thine
In thy soul's thought, all naked, will bestow it,
Till whatsoever star that guides my moving
Points on me graciously with fair aspect,
And puts apparel on my tattered loving,
To show me worthy of thy great respect.

SONNET 26, 1-12

### WORTHY OF RESPECT

God's works are so great, worth
A lifetime of study—endless enjoyment!
Splendor and beauty mark his craft;
His generosity never gives out.
His miracles are his memorial—
This God of Grace, this God of Love.
He gave food to those who fear him,
He remembered to keep his ancient promise.
He proved to his people that he could do what he said:
Hand them the nations on a platter—a gift!
He manufactures truth and justice;
All his products are guaranteed to last—
Never out-of-date, never obsolete, rust-proof.
All that he makes and does is honest and true:
He paid the ransom for his people,
He ordered his Covenant kept forever.
He's so personal and holy, worthy of our respect.
The good life begins in the fear of God—
Do that and you'll know the blessing of God.

PSALM 111:2-10

### KISS ME

*Romeo:*
If I profane with my unworthiest hand
This holy shrine, the gentle sin is this,
My lips, two blushing pilgrims, ready stand
To smooth that rough touch with a tender kiss.

*Juliet:*
Good pilgrim, you do wrong your hand too much,
Which mannerly devotion shows in this:
For saints have hands that pilgrims' hands do touch,
And palm to palm is holy palmers' kiss.

*Romeo:*
Have not saints lips, and holy palmers, too?

*Juliet:*
Ay, pilgrim, lips that they must use in prayer.

*Romeo:*
O then, dear saint, let lips do what hands do,
They pray—grant thou, lest faith turn to despair.

*Juliet:*
Saints do not move, though grant for prayers' sake.

**ROMEO AND JULIET, I. V. 93-105**

### KISS ME

*The Woman:*
*Kiss me—full on the mouth!*
> *Yes! For your love is better than wine,*
> *headier than your aromatic oils.*
*The syllables of your name murmur like a meadow brook.*
> *No wonder everyone loves to say your name!*

*The Man:*
*Your lips are jewel red,*
> *your mouth elegant and inviting,*
> *your veiled cheeks soft and radiant....*

*The sweet, fragrant curves of your body,*
> *The soft, spiced contours of your flesh*
*Invite me, and I come. I stay*
> *until dawn breathes its light and night slips away.*

SONG OF SONGS 1:2-3, 4:3, 6

### ENCORES TO THE END OF TIME

Let me not to the marriage of true minds
Admit impediments; love is not love
Which alters when it alteration finds,
Or bends with the remover to remove.
O no, it is an ever-fixed mark
That looks on tempests and is never shaken;
It is the star to every wandering bark....

SONNET 116, 1-7

### ENCORES TO THE END OF TIME

*Everything in the world is about to be wrapped up, so take nothing for granted. Stay wide-awake in prayer. Most of all, love each other as if your life depended on it. Love makes up for practically anything. Be quick to give a meal to the hungry, a bed to the homeless—cheerfully. Be generous with the different things God gave you, passing them around so all get in on it: if words, let it be God's words; if help, let it be God's hearty help. That way, God's bright presence will be evident in everything through Jesus, and he'll get all the credit as the One mighty in everything—encores to the end of time. Oh, yes!*

I PETER 4:7-11

### AWAKEN MY LOVE

Love comforteth like sunshine after rain,
But lust's effect is tempest after sun;
Love's gentle spring doth always fresh remain;
Lust's winter comes ere summer half be done;
Love surfeits not, lust like a glutton dies.
Love is all truth, lust full of forged lies.

VENUS AND ADONIS, 799-804

### AWAKEN MY LOVE

*"Blessed are you, God of our fathers! Blessed be your name forever and ever! May the heavens and all your creatures bless you from age to age! You made Adam and gave him Eve. From both came the human race. You said, did you not, that it was not good for man to be alone? That he needed a helper, a look-alike? And so you provided. Now I take this woman, my cousin, as my lawful wife, not to quiet my lust but to awaken my love. Keep our best interests at heart. We want to have children and grow old together."*

*"Amen," he said, and "Amen," she said.*

*Back to be they went and continued the betrothal sequence they'd interrupted for the prayer.*

TOBIT 8:5-9

### SINLESS IN GOD'S SIGHT?

So oft it chances in particular men,
That for some vicious mole of nature in them…
These men, carrying, I say, the stamp of one defect,
Being nature's livery, or fortunes star,
His virtues else, be they pure as grace,
As infinite as man may undergo,
Shall in the general censure take corruption
From that particular fault: the dram of evil
Doth all the noble substance of a doubt
To his own scandal.

HAMLET, I. iv. 23-24, 30-38

### SINLESS IN GOD'S SIGHT?

*Look at you! You trivialize religion,*
  *turn spiritual conversation into empty gossip....*
*Do you think you're the first person to have*
      *to deal with these things?*
  *Have you been around as long as the hills?*
*Were you listening in when God planned all this?*
  *Do you think you're the only one who knows anything?*
*What do you know that we don't know?*
  *What insights do you have that we've missed?*
*Gray beards and white hair back us up—*
  *old folks who've been around a lot longer than you.*
*Are God's promises not enough for you,*
  *spoken so gently and tenderly?*
*Why do you let your emotions take over,*
  *lashing out and spitting fire,*
*Pitting your whole being against God*
  *by letting words like this come out of your mouth?*
*Do you think it's possible for any mere mortal to be sinless*
      *in God's sight,*
  *for anyone born of a human mother to get it all together?*
*Why, God can't even trust his holy angels.*
  *He sees the flaws in the very heavens themselves,*
*So how much less we humans, smelly and foul,*
  *who lap up evil like water?*

JOB 15:4, 7-16

### THE LIFE-LIGHT

Ay me! For aught that I could ever read…
If there were a sympathy in choice,
War, death, or sickness did lay siege to it,
Making it momentary as a sound,
Swift as a shadow, short as any dream,
Brief as the lightening in the collied night,
That, in a spleen, unfolds both Heaven and Earth,
And ere a man hath power to say, "Behold!"
The jaws of darkness do devour it up:
So quick bright things come to confusion.

A MIDSUMMER NIGHT'S DREAM, I. i. 132, 141-149

### THE LIFE-LIGHT

The Word was first,
    the Word present to God,
God present to the Word.
The Word was God,
    in readiness for God from day one.

Everything was created through him;
    nothing—not one thing!—
    came into being without him.
What came into existence was Life,
    and the Life was Light to live by.
The Life-Light blazed out of the darkness;
    the darkness couldn't put it out.

JOHN 1:1-5

### GOD ALWAYS GETS BLAMED

This is the excellent foppery of the world, that when we are sick in fortune—often the surfeit of our own behavior—we make guilty of our disasters the sun, the moon, and the stars; as if we were villains by necessity, fools by heavenly compulsion, knaves, thieves, and treachers by spherical predominance; drunkards, liars, and adulterers by enforc'd obedience of planetary influence; and all that we are evil in, by a divine thrusting on.

KING LEAR, I. ii. 118-126

## GOD ALWAYS GETS BLAMED

*People ruin their lives by their own stupidity,*
*so why does GOD always get blamed?*

PROVERBS 19:3

### TRUTH FROM THE INSIDE OUT

Canst thou not minister to my mind diseas'd,
Pluck from the memory a rooted sorrow,
Raze out the written troubles of the brain,
And with some sweet oblivious antidote
Cleanse the stuff'd bosom of that perilous stuff
Which weighs upon the heart?

MACBETH, V. iii. 40-44

### TRUTH FROM THE INSIDE OUT

*Generous in love—God, give grace!*
    *Huge in mercy—wipe out my bad record.*
*Scrub away my guilt,*
    *soak out my sins in your laundry.*
*I know how bad I've been;*
    *my sins are staring me down.*

*You're the One I've violated, and you've seen*
    *it all, seen the full extent of my evil.*
*You have all the facts before you;*
    *whatever you decide about me is fair.*
*I've been out of step with you for a long time,*
    *in the wrong since before I was born.*
*What you're after is truth from the inside out.*
    *Enter me, then; conceive a new, true life.*

PSALM 51:1-6

### THE GOD-REVEALER

In the corrupted currents of this world
Offence's gilded hand may shove by justice,
And oft 'tis seen the wicked prize itself
Buys out the law, but 'tis not so above:
There is no shuffling, there the action lies
In his true nature, and we ourselves compelled
Even to the teeth and forehead of our faults,
To give evidence. What then? What rests?
Try what repentance can. What can it not?
Yet what can it, when one cannot repent?
O wretched state! O bosom black as death!
O limed soul, that struggling to be free
Art more engag'd. Help, angels! Make assay,
Bow, stubborn knees, and heart, with strings of steel,
Be soft as sinews of the newborn babe.
All may be well....

HAMLET, III. iii. 57-71

### THE GOD-REVEALER

*The very next day John saw Jesus coming toward him and yelled out, "Here he is, God's Passover Lamb! He forgives the sins of the world! This is the man I've been talking about, 'the One who comes after me but is really ahead of me.' I knew nothing about who he was—only this: that my task has been to get Israel ready to recognize him as the God-Revealer. That is why I came here baptizing with water, giving you a good bath and scrubbing sins from your life so you can get a fresh start with God."*

*John clinched his witness with this: "I watched the Spirit, like a dove flying down out of the sky, making himself at home in him. I repeat, I know nothing about him except this: The One who authorized me to baptize with water told me, 'The One on whom you see the Spirit come down and stay, this One will baptize with the Holy Spirit.' That's exactly what I saw happen, and I'm telling you, there's no question about it: This is the Son of God."*

JOHN 1:29-34

### FOR THE BENEFIT OF ALL

There is a tide in the affairs of men,
Which taken at the flood, leads on to fortune;
Omitted, all the voyage of their life
Is bound in shallows and in miseries.
On such a full sea are we now afloat,
And we must take the current when it serves,
Or lose our ventures.

JULIUS CAESAR, IV. iii. 218-224

## FOR THE BENEFIT OF ALL

*So let's not allow ourselves to get fatigued doing good. At the right time we will harvest a good crop if we don't give up, or quit. Right now, therefore, every time we get the chance, let us work for the benefit of all, starting with the people closest to us in the community of faith.*

GALATIANS 6:9-10

### ALL WE ASK

O God of battles, steel my soldiers' hearts,
Possess them not with fear! Take from them now
The sense of reckoning, if the opposed numbers
Pluck their hearts from them. Not today, O Lord,
O, not today, think not upon the fault
My father made in compassing the crown!...
Five hundred poor I have in yearly pay,
Who twice a day their withered hands hold up
Toward Heaven, to pardon blood; and I have built
Two chantries, where sad and solemn priests
Sing still for Richard's soul. More will I do;
Though all that I can do is nothing worth,
Since that my penitence comes after all,
Imploring pardon.

HENRY THE FIFTH, IV. i. 288-294, 298-305

### ALL WE ASK

*When that year was over, the next year rolled around and they were back, saying, "Master, it's no secret to you that we're broke: our money's gone and we've traded you all our livestock. We've nothing left to barter with but our bodies and our farms. What use are our bodies and our land if we stand here and starve to death right in front of you? Trade us food for our bodies and our land. We'll be slaves to Pharaoh and give up our land—all we ask is seed for survival, just enough to live on and keep the farms alive."*

GENESIS 47:18-19

### AFTER YOU'VE BEEN KING

For within the hollow crown
That rounds the mortal temples of a king
Keeps Death his court, and there the antic sits,
Scoffing his state and grinning at his pomp,
Allowing him a breath,  a little scene,
To monarchize, be feared, and kill with looks,
Infusing him with self and vain conceit,
As if this flesh which walls about our life
Were brass impregnable; and humor'd thus,
Comes at last, and with a little pin,
Bores through his castle wall, and farewell king!

RICHARD THE SECOND, III. ii. 160-170

### AFTER YOU'VE BEEN KING

*Then I took a good look at everything I'd done, looked at all the sweat and hard work. But when I looked, I saw nothing but smoke. Smoke and spitting into the wind. There was nothing to any of it. Nothing.*

*And then I took a hard look at what's smart and what's stupid. What's left to do after you've been king? That's a hard act to follow. You just do what you can, and that's it. But I did see that it's better to be smart than stupid, just as light is better than darkness. Even so, though the smart ones see where they're going and the stupid ones grope in the dark, they're all the same in the end. One fate for all—and that's it.*

*When I realized that my fate's the same as the fool's, I had to ask myself, "So why bother being wise?" It's all smoke, nothing but smoke. The smart and the stupid both disappear out of sight. In a day or two they're both forgotten. Yes, both the smart and the stupid die, and that's it.*

ECCLESIASTES 2:11-16

### THE HARDER THE FALL

Could great men thunder
As Jove himself does, Jove would never be quiet,
For every pelting, petty officer
Would use his Heaven for thunder,
Nothing but thunder! Merciful Heaven,
Thou rather with thy sharp and sulphurous bolt
Splits the unwedgeable and gnarled oak
Than the soft myrtle. But Man, proud Man,
Dressed in a little brief authority,
Most ignorant of what he's most assured,
His glassy essence, like an angry ape
Plays such fantastic tricks before high Heaven
As makes the angels weep, who, with our spleens,
Would all themselves laugh mortal.

**MEASURE FOR MEASURE, II. ii. 110-123**

## THE HARDER THE FALL

*First pride, then the crash—*
*the bigger the ego, the harder the fall.*

PROVERBS 16:18

### THE VARIABLES IN GOVERNING

Love thyself last, cherish those hearts that hate thee;
Corruption wins not more than honesty.
Still in thy right hand carry gentle peace
To silence envious tongues. Be just, and fear not;
Let all the ends thou aim'st at be thy country's,
Thy God's, and truth's; then if thou fall'st, O Cromwell,
Thou fall'st a blessed martyr.

HENRY THE EIGHTH, III. ii. 443-449

### THE VARIABLES IN GOVERNING

*Xerxes, the great king from India to Ethiopia, 127 provinces with governors and all others who respect our authority, wishes you well.*

*Many who have enjoyed the king's bountiful generosity have abused the king's authority. Not only do they seek to oppress his subjects but they also plot against the very one who gave them the authority in the first place. They downgrade the good things people do; they even upgrade the evil thing they themselves do by thing them not so bad.*

*Many in positions of importance, with the help of local officials, become accomplices to attempted extermination. These are the sort of persons who look for loopholes in a good law, when they want to pursue their own unlawful ends. We do not have to harken back to incidents in ancient history for crimes committed by people while they were in office. We have only to recall crimes committed in our own time.*

*From now on we shall make peace a top priority in all the provinces. If we pay attention to the variables in governing, we will err more on the good side than the bad.*

ESTHER 8:12D-12L (AKA 16:1-9)

## NO END TO GOD'S SURPRISES

The quality of mercy is not strain'd,
It droppeth as the gentle rain from Heaven
Upon the place beneath. It is twice blest:
It blesseth him that gives and him that takes.
'Tis mightiest in the mightiest, it becomes
The throned monarch better than his crown.
His scepter shows the force of temporal power,
The attribute to awe and majesty,
Wherein doth sit the dread and fear of kings;
But mercy is above this sceptered sway,
It is enthroned in the hearts if kings,
It is an attribute to God himself;
And earthly power doth then show likest God's
When mercy seasons justice.

THE MERCHANT OF VENICE, IV. i. 184-197

### NO END TO GOD'S SURPRISES

*If I were in your shoes, I'd go straight to God,*
    *I'd throw myself on the mercy of God.*
*After all, he's famous for great and unexpected acts;*
    *there's no end to his surprises.*
*He gives rain, for instance, across the wide earth,*
    *sends water to irrigate the fields.*
*He raises up the down-and-out,*
    *gives firm footing to those sinking in grief.*
*He aborts the schemes of conniving crooks,*
    *so that none of their plots come to term.*
*He catches the know-it-alls in their conspiracies—*
    *all that intricate intrigue swept out with the trash!*
*Suddenly they're disoriented, plunged into darkness;*
    *they can't see to put one foot in front of the other.*
*But the downtrodden are saved by God,*
    *saved from the murderous plots, saved from the iron fist.*
*And so the poor continue to hope,*
    *while injustice is bound and gagged.*

JOB 5:8-16

### DON'T RUN FROM SUFFERING

All the places that the eye of Heaven visits
Are to a wise man ports and happy havens.
Teach thy necessity to reason thus:
There is no virtue like necessity.
Think not the King did banish thee,
But thou the King.

RICHARD THE SECOND, I. iii. 275-280

### DON'T RUN FROM SUFFERING

*"Don't run from suffering; embrace it. Follow me and I'll show you how. Self-help is no help at all. Self-sacrifice is the way, my way, to finding yourself, your true self. What good would it do to get everything you want and lose you, the real you? If any of you is embarrassed with me and the way I'm leading you, know that the Son of Man will be far more embarrassed with you when he arrives in all his splendor in company with the Father and the holy angels. This isn't, you realize, pie in the sky by and by. Some who have taken their stand right here are going to see it happen, see with their own eyes the kingdom of God."*

LUKE 9:24-27

### YOU WERE STRANGERS

Imagine that you see the wretched strangers,
Their babies at their backs, with their poor luggage
Plodding to the ports and coasts for transportation,
And that you sit as kings in your desires....
You'll put down strangers?
Kill them? Cut their throats? Possess their houses?
Alas, alas, say now the King,
As he is clement if the offender mourn,
Should so much come too short of your great trespass
As but to banish you. Wither would you go?
What country by the nature of your error
Should give you harbor?...
Why you must needs be strangers.
Would you be pleased
To find a nation of such barbarous temper
That breaking out in hideous violence
Would not afford you an abode on earth,
Whet their detested knives against you throat,
Spurn you like dogs, and like as if that God
Owed not, nor made not you, nor that the elements
Were not all appropriate to your comforts,
But chartered unto them? What would you think
To be thus used? This is the strangers case,
And this your mountainous inhumanity.

SIR THOMAS MORE, II. iv. 74-77; 119-127, 130-140

66

## YOU WERE STRANGERS

*"Don't take advantage of a stranger. You know what it's like to be a stranger; you were strangers in Egypt."*

EXODUS 23:9

## OVERLOOKED OR IGNORED

Poor naked wretches, whereso'er you are,
That bide the pelting of this pitiless storm,
How shall your houseless heads and unfed sides,
Your looped and windowed raggedness, defend you
From seasons such as these? O, I have ta'en
Too little care of this! Take physic pomp,
Expose thyself to feel what wretches feel,
That thou mayst shake the superflux to them,
And show the Heavens more just.

KING LEAR, III. iv. 28-36

### OVERLOOKED OR IGNORED

"Then the King will say to those on his right, 'Enter, you who are blessed by my Father! Take what's coming to you in this kingdom. It's been ready for you since the world's foundation. And here's why:

> I was hungry and you fed me,
> I was thirsty and you gave me a drink,
> I was homeless and you gave me a room,
> I was shivering and you gave me clothes,
> I was sick and you stopped to visit,
> I was in prison and you came to me.'

"Then those 'sheep' are going to say, 'Master, what are you talking about? When did we ever see you hungry and feed you, thirsty and give you a drink? And when did we ever see you sick or in prison and come to you?' Then the King will say, 'I'm telling the solemn truth: Whenever you did one of these things to someone overlooked or ignored, that was me—you did it to me.'"

MATTHEW 25:34-40

### BE CONTENT WITH OBSCURITY

When in disgrace with Fortune and men's eyes
I all alone beweep my out cast state,
And trouble deaf Heaven with my bootless cries,
And look upon myself and curse my fate,
Wishing me like to one more rich in hope,
Featured like him, like him with friends possess'd,
Desiring this man's art and that man's scope,
With what I most enjoy contented least;
Yet, in these thoughts myself almost despising,
Haply I think on thee, and then my state
Like to the lark at break of day arising
From sullen earth, sings hymns at Heaven's gate;
For thy sweet love remembered such wealth brings
That then I scorn to change my state with kings.

SONNET 29

## BE CONTENT WITH OBSCURITY

*So if you're serious about living this new resurrection life with Christ, act like it. Pursue the things over which Christ presides. Don't shuffle along, eyes to the ground, absorbed with the things right in front of you. Look up, and be alert to what is going on around Christ—that's where the action is. See things from his perspective.*

*Your old life is dead. Your new life, which is your real life—even though invisible to spectators—is with Christ in God. He is your life. When Christ (your real life, remember) shows up again on this earth, you'll show up, too—the real you, the glorious you. Meanwhile, be content with obscurity, like Christ.*

COLOSSIANS 3:1-4

### THE WILLING HUMBLE

Come let's away to prison:
We two alone will sing like birds i'th' cage.
When thou dost ask me blessing, I'll kneel down
And ask of thee forgiveness. So we'll live,
And pray, and sing, and tell old tales, and laugh
At gilded butterflies, and hear poor rogues
Talk of court news; and we'll talk with them, too,
Who loses and who wins; who's in, who's out—
And take upon us the mystery of things
As if we were God's spies; and we'll wear out
In a wall'd prison, packs and sects of great ones,
That ebb and flow by th' moon.

KING LEAR, V. iii. 8-18

### THE WILLING HUMBLE

*You're cheating on God. If all you want is your own way, flirting with the world every chance you get, you end up enemies of God and his way. And do you suppose God doesn't care? The proverb has it that "he's a fiercely jealous lover." And what he gives in love is far better than anything else you'll find. It's common knowledge that "God goes against the willful proud; God gives grace to the willing humble."*

JAMES 4:4-6

## NO ONE CAN CONTROL THE WIND

Blow, blow, thou winter wind!
Thou art not so unkind
As man's ingratitude;
Thy tooth is not so keen,
Because thou art not seen,
Although thy breath be rude.
Heigh-ho! Sing, heigh-ho! unto the green holly,
Most friendship is feigning, most loving mere folly.
Then heigh-ho, the holly!
This life is most jolly.

AS YOU LIKE IT, II. vii. 174-183

### NO ONE CAN CONTROL THE WIND

*No one can control the wind or lock it in a box.*
*No one has any say-so regarding the day of death.*
*No one can stop a battle in its tracks.*
*No one who does evil can be saved by evil.*

*All this I observed as I tried my best to understand all that's going on in this world. As long as men and women have the power to hurt each other, this is the way it is.*

ECCLESIASTES 8:8-9

### A GREAT AND JOYFUL EVENT

Some say that ever 'gainst that Season comes
Wherein our Savior's birth is celebrated
The bird of dawning singeth all night long;
And then, they say, no spirit can walk abroad,
The nights are wholesome; then no planets strike,
No fairy takes, nor witch hath power to charm,
So hallowed and so gracious is th' time.

HAMLET, I. i. 158-164

### A GREAT AND JOYFUL EVENT

There were sheepherders camping in the neighborhood. They had set night watches over their sheep. Suddenly, God's angel stood among them and God's glory blazed around them. They were terrified. The angel said, "Don't be afraid. I'm here to announce a great and joyful event that is meant for everybody, worldwide: A Savior has just been born in David's town, a Savior who is Messiah and Master. This is what you're to look for: a baby wrapped in a blanket and lying in a manger."

At once the angel was joined by a huge angelic choir singing God's praises:

Glory to God in the heavenly heights,
Peace to all men and women on earth who please him.

As the angel choir withdrew into heaven, the sheepherders talked it over. "Let's get over to Bethlehem as fast as we can and see for ourselves what God has revealed to us." They left, running, and found Mary and Joseph, and the baby lying in the manger. Seeing was believing. They told everyone they met what the angels had said about this child. All who heard the sheepherders were impressed.

Mary kept all these things to herself, holding them dear, deep within herself. The sheepherders returned and let loose, glorifying and praising God for everything they had heard and seen. It turned out exactly the way they'd been told!

LUKE 2:8-20

### THE GOD-COLORS IN THE WORLD

O, thou clear God, and Patron of all light,
From whom each lamp and shining star doth borrow
The beauteous influence that makes him bright,
There lives a Son that suck'd an earthly Mother
May lend thee light, as thou doth lend another.

**VENUS AND ADONIS, 860-864**

### THE GOD-COLORS IN THE WORLD

"Here's another way to put it: You're here to be light, bringing out the God-colors in the world. God is not a secret to be kept. We're going public with this, as public as a city on a hill. If I make you light-bearers, you don't think I'm going to hide you under a bucket, do you? I'm putting you on a light stand. Now that I've put you there on a hilltop, on a light stand—shine! Keep open house; be generous with your lives. By opening up to others, you'll prompt people to open up with God, this generous Father in heaven."

MATTHEW 5:14-16

### ALL THAT'S LEFT NOW

Fear no more the heat o' th' sun,
Nor the furious winter's rages,
Thou thy worldly task hast done,
Home art gone, and ta'en thy wages.
Golden lads and girls all must,
As chimney-sweepers, come to dust.

Fear no more the frown o' th' great,
Thou art past the tyrant's stroke;
Care no more to clothe and eat,
To thee the reed is as the oak.
The scepter, learning, physic, must
All follow this and come to dust.

Fear no more the lightning-flash,
Nor th' all-dreaded thunder-stone.
Fear not slander, censure rash.
Thou hast finished joy and moan.
All lovers young, all lovers must
Consign to thee and come to dust.

CYMBELINE, IV. ii. 258-275

### ALL THAT'S LEFT NOW

*You take over. I'm about to die, my life an offering on God's altar. This is the only race worth running. I've run hard right to the finish, believed all the way. All that's left now is the shouting—God's applause! Depend on it, he's an honest judge. He'll do right not only by me, but by everyone eager for his coming.*

2 TIMOTHY 4:6-8

### THE WHOLE WORLD'S A CHOIR

Hark, hark, the lark at Heaven's gate sings!
And Pheobus begins arise,
His steeds to water at those springs
On chaliced flowers that lies;
And winking Mary-buds begin to ope their golden eyes:
With every thing that pretty is, my Lady sweet, arise.
Arise, arise!

CYMBELINE, II. iii. 20-26

### THE WHOLE WORLD'S A CHOIR

*Get up, my dear friend,*
    *fair and beautiful lover—come to me!*
*Look around you: Winter is over;*
    *the winter rains are over, gone!*
*Spring flowers are in blossom all over.*
    *The whole world's a choir—and singing!*
*Spring warblers are filling the forest*
    *with sweet arpeggios.*
*Lilacs are exuberantly purple and perfumed,*
    *and cherry trees fragrant with blossoms.*
*Oh, get up, dear friend,*
    *my fair and beautiful lover—come to me!*
*Come, my shy and modest dove—*
    *leave your seclusion, come out in the open.*
*Let me see your face,*
    *let me hear your voice.*
*For your voice is soothing*
    *and your face is ravishing.*

SONG OF SONGS 2:10-14

### EARTH, NEW-CREATED

Our revels now are ended. These our actors,
As I foretold you, were all spirits, and
Are melted into air, into thin air;
And like the baseless fabric of this vision,
The cloud-capped towers, the gorgeous palaces,
The solemn temples, the great globe itself,
Yea, all which it inherit, shall dissolve,
And like this insubstantial pageant faded,
Leave not a rack behind. We are such stuff
As dreams are made on; and our little life
Is rounded with a sleep.

THE TEMPEST, IV. i. 148-158

### EARTH, NEW-CREATED

*I saw Heaven and earth new-created. Gone the first Heaven, gone the first earth, gone the sea.*

*I saw Holy Jerusalem, new-created, descending resplendent out of Heaven, as ready for God as a bride for her husband.*

*I heard a voice thunder from the Throne: "Look! Look! God has moved into the neighborhood, making his home with men and women! They're his people, he's their God. He'll wipe every tear from their eyes. Death is gone for good—tears gone, crying gone, pain gone—all the first order of things gone." The Enthroned continued, "Look! I'm making everything new. Write it all down—each word dependable and accurate."*

### REVELATION 21:1-5

### FALLING APART

Ay, but to die, and go we know not where;
To lie in cold obstruction, and to rot;
This sensible warm motion to become
A kneaded clod; and the delighted spirit
To bathe in fiery floods, or to reside
In thrilling region of thick-ribbed ice;
To be imprison'd in the viewless winds
And blown with restless violence round about
The pendant world....
The weariest and most loathed worldly life
That age, ache, penury, and imprisonment
Can lay on nature is a Paradise
To what we fear of death.

MEASURE FOR MEASURE,
III. i. 117-125, 128-131

### FALLING APART

*Jesus told them, "You're all going to feel that your world is falling apart and that it's my fault. There's a Scripture that says,*

> *I will strike the shepherd;*
> *The sheep will go helter-skelter.*

*"But after I am raised up, I will go ahead of you, leading the way to Galilee."*

MARK 14:27-28

### WE'LL ALL BE CHANGED

Not a whit, we defy augury. There is special providence in the fall of a sparrow. If it be now, 'tis not to come; if it be not to come, it will be now; if it be not now, yet it will come. The readiness is all. Since no man has aught of what he leaves, what is't to leave betimes. Let be.

HAMLET, V. ii. 219-224

### WE'LL ALL BE CHANGED

*But let me tell you something wonderful, a mystery I'll probably never fully understand. We're not all going to die— but we are all going to be changed. You hear a blast to end all blasts from a trumpet, and in the time that you look up and blink your eyes—it's over. On signal from that trumpet from heaven, the dead will be up and out of their graves, beyond the reach of death, never to die again. At the same moment and in the same way, we'll all be changed. In the resurrection scheme of things, this has to happen: everything perishable taken off the shelves and replaced by the imperishable, this mortal replaced by the immortal. Then the saying will come true:*

> *Death swallowed by triumphant Life!*
> *Who got the last word, oh, Death?*
> *Oh, Death, who's afraid of you now?*

*It was sin that made death so frightening and law-code guilt that gave sin its leverage, its destructive power. But now in a single victorious stroke of Life, all three—sin, guilt, death— are gone, the gift of our Master, Jesus Christ. Thank God!*

I CORINTHIANS 15:51-57

89

### THE POINT OF LIFE

Be absolute for death: either death or life
Shall thereby be the sweeter. Reason thus with life:
If I do lose thee, I do lose a thing
That none but fools would keep. A breath thou art,
Servile to all skyey influences,
That this habitation where thou keep'st
Hourly afflict.

**MEASURE FOR MEASURE, III. i. 5-11**

### THE POINT OF LIFE

*"Why does God bother giving light to the miserable,*
*    why bother keeping bitter people alive,*
*Those who want in the worst way to die, and can't,*
*    who can't imagine anything better than death,*
*Who count the day of their death and burial*
*    the happiest day of their life?*
*What's the point of life when it doesn't make sense,*
*    when God blocks all the roads to meaning?"*

JOB 3:20-23

## WEEPING AND MUCH LAMENT

Grief fills the room up of my absent child,
Lies in his bed, walks up and down with me,
Puts on his pretty looks, repeats his words,
Remembers me of all his gracious parts,
Stuffs out his vacant garments with his form....
O Lord, my boy, my Arthur, my fair son!
My life, my joy, my food, my all the world.

KING JOHN, III. iv. 93-97, 102-104

### WEEPING AND MUCH LAMENT

*Herod, when he realized that the scholars had tricked him, flew into a rage. He commanded the murder of every little boy two years old and under who lived in Bethlehem and its surrounding hills. (He determined that age from information he'd gotten from the scholars.) That's when Jeremiah's sermon was fulfilled:*

> *A sound was heard in Ramah,*
> > *weeping and much lament.*
> *Rachel weeping for her children,*
> > *Rachel refusing all solace,*
> *Her children gone,*
> > *dead and buried.*

MATTHEW 2:16-18

### I'LL BE THERE SOON

Come, gentle night, come, loving, black-brow'd night,
Give me my Romeo, and, when I shall die,
Take him and cut him out in little stars,
And he will make the face of heaven so fine
That all the world will be in love with night,
And pay no worship to the garish sun.

ROMEO AND JULIET, III. ii. 20-25

I'LL BE THERE SOON

*He who testifies to all these things says it again: "I'm on my way! I'll be there soon!"*

*Yes! Come, Master Jesus!*
*The grace of the Master Jesus be with all of you.*
*Oh, Yes!*

REVELATION 22:20-21

### SAFE PASSAGE

Let us be back'd with God, and with the seas
Which He hath giv'n for fence impregnable,
And with their helps only defend ourselves.
In them, and in ourselves, our safety lies.

**HENRY THE SIXTH, PART THREE, IV. i. 43-46**

### SAFE PASSAGE

*The seventy came back triumphant. "Master, even the demons danced to your tune!"*

*Jesus said, "I know. I saw Satan fall, a bolt of lightning out of the sky. See what I've given you? Safe passage as you walk on snakes and scorpions, and protection from every assault of the Enemy. No one can put a hand on you. All the same, the great triumph is not in your authority over evil, but in God's authority over you and presence with you. Not what you do for God but what God does for you—that's the agenda for rejoicing."*

LUKE 10:17-20

### DESPERATE FOR A CHANGE

Are not these woods
More free from peril than the envious court?
Here feel we not the penalty of Adam,
The seasons' difference, as the icy fang
And churlish chiding of the winter's wind,
Which, when it bites and blows upon my body
Even till I shrink with cold, I smile and say,
"This is no flattery; these are counselors
That feelingly persuade me what I am."
Sweet are the uses of adversity,
Which like the toad, ugly and venomous,
Wears yet a precious jewel in his head;
And this our life, exempt from public haunt,
Finds tongues in trees, books in the running brooks,
Sermons in stones, and good in everything.

AS YOU LIKE IT, II. i. 3-17

### DESPERATE FOR A CHANGE

*My insides are turned inside out;*
    *specters of death have me down.*
*I shake with fear,*
    *I shudder from head to foot.*
*"Who will give me wings," I ask—*
    *"wings like a dove?"*
*Get me out of here on dove wings;*
    *I want some peace and quiet.*
*I want a walk in the country,*
    *I want a cabin in the woods.*
*I'm desperate for a change*
    *from rage and stormy weather.*

PSALM 55:4-8

### BE IN PRAYER

Now my charms are all o'erthrown
And what strength I have's mine own,
Which is most faint. Now, 'tis true,
I must be here confin'd by you,
Or sent to Naples. Let me not,
Since I have my dukedom got,
And pardoned the deceiver, dwell
In this bare island by your spell,
But release me from my bands
With the help of your good hands.
Gentle breath of yours my sails
Must fill, or else my project fails,
Which was to please. Now I want
Spirits to enforce, art to enchant,
And my ending is despair,
Unless I be relieved by prayer,
Which pierces so, that it assaults
Mercy itself, and frees all faults.
As you from crimes would pardoned be,
Let your indulgence set me free.

**THE TEMPEST, EPILOGUE**

### BE IN PRAYER

*Then Jesus went with them to a garden called Gethsemane and told his disciples, "Stay here while I go over there and pray." Taking along Peter and the two sons of Zebedee, he plunged into an agonizing sorrow. Then he said, "This sorrow is crushing my life out. Stay here and keep vigil with me."*

*Going a little ahead, he fell on his face, praying, "My Father, if there is any way, get me out of this. But please, not what I want. You, what do you want?"*

*When he came back to his disciples, he found them sound asleep. He said to Peter, "Can't you stick it out with me a single hour? Stay alert; be in prayer so you don't wander into temptation without even knowing you're in danger. There is a part of you that is eager, ready for anything in God. But there's another part that's as lazy as an old dog sleeping by the fire."*

MATTHEW 26:36-41

### PRAY VERY SIMPLY

But, yet like prayers divine,
I must each day say o'er the very same,
Counting no old thing old, thou mine, I thine,
Even as first I hallowed Thy fair name.

SONNET 108, 5-8

### PRAY VERY SIMPLY

"The world is full of so-called prayer warriors who are prayer-ignorant. They're full of formulas and programs and advice, peddling techniques for getting what you want from God. Don't fall for that nonsense. This is your Father you are dealing with, and he knows better than you what you need. With a God like this loving you, you can pray very simply. Like this:

*Our Father in heaven,*
*Reveal who you are.*
*Set the world right;*
*Do what's best—*
 *as above, so below.*
*Keep us alive with three square meals.*
*Keep us forgiven with you and forgiving others.*
*Keep us safe from ourselves and the Devil.*
*You're in charge!*
*You can do anything you want!*
*You're ablaze in beauty!*
 *Yes. Yes. Yes.*"

MATTHEW 6:7-13

### IT'S STILL THERE TODAY

Good friends, for Jesus' sake, forbear
To dig the dust enclosed here.
Blest be the man that spares these stones
And curst be he that moves my bones.

EPITAPH ON WILLIAM SHAKESPEARE'S GRAVE
HOLY TRINITY CHURCH, STRATFORD-UPON-AVON

Would that some good angel might roll the stone away,
And thy form come forth in the Saviour's likeness!
But my prayers avail not. Come quickly, O, Christ!
Then shall my mother, though enclosed in the tomb,
Arise and mount to heaven.

EPITAPH OF SHAKESPEARE'S WIFE, ANNE HATHAWAY
HOLY TRINITY CHURCH, STRATFORD-UPON-AVON

### IT'S STILL THERE TODAY

*Rachel died and was buried on the road to Ephrath, that is, Bethlehem. Jacob set up a pillar to mark her grave. It is still there today, "Rachel's Grave Stone."*

GENESIS 35:19-20

### EMBRACE AND KISS

Beauty, Truth, and Rarity,
Grace in all simplicity,
Here enclos'd, in cinders lie.

Death is now the Phoenix' nest,
And the Turtle's loyal breast
To eternity doth rest.

Truth may seem, but cannot be;
Beauty brag, but 'tis not she;
Truth and beauty buried be.

To this urn let those repair
That are either true or fair;
For these dead birds sigh a prayer.

THE PHOENIX AND TURTLE, 53-58, 62-67

### EMBRACE AND KISS

*Love and Truth meet in the street,*
  *Right Living and Whole Living embrace and kiss!*
*Truth sprouts green from the ground,*
  *Right Living pours down from the skies!*
*Oh yes! GOD gives Goodness and Beauty;*
  *our land responds with Bounty and Blessing.*
*Right Living strides out before him,*
  *and clears a path for his passage.*

PSALM 85:10-13

### THE GLORY-STRENGTH GOD GIVES

Now with the drops of this most balmy time
My love looks fresh, and Death to me subscribes,
Since spite of him I'll live in this poor rhyme,
While he insults o'er dull and speechless tribes;
And thou in this shalt find thy monument,
When tyrants' crests and tombs of brass are spent.

SONNET 107, 9-14

### THE GLORY-STRENGTH GOD GIVES

*The Message is as true among you today as when you first heard it. It doesn't diminish or weaken over time. It's the same all over the world. The Message bears fruit and gets larger and stronger, just as it has in you. From the very first day you heard and recognized the truth of what God is doing, you've been hungry for more. It's as vigorous in you now as when you learned it from our friend and close associate Epaphras. He is one reliable worker for Christ! I could always depend on him. He's the one who told us how thoroughly love had been worked into your lives by the Spirit.*

*Be assured that from the first day we heard of you, we haven't stopped praying for you, asking God to give you wise minds and spirits attuned to his will, and so acquire a thorough understanding of the ways in which God works. We pray that you'll live well for the Master, making him proud of you as you work hard in his orchard. As you learn more and more how God works, you will learn how to do your work. We pray that you'll have the strength to stick it out over the long haul—not the grim strength of gritting your teeth but the glory-strength God gives. It is strength that endures the unendurable and spills over into joy, thanking the Father who makes us strong enough to take part in everything bright and beautiful that he has for us.*

COLOSSIANS 1:5-12

### LOVE NEVER DIES

Love's not Time's fool, though rosy lips and cheeks
Within his bending sickle's compass come;
Love alters not with his brief hours and weeks,
But bears it out even till the edge of doom.
If this be error and upon me proved,
I never writ, nor no man ever loved.

SONNET 116, 9-14

## LOVE NEVER DIES

*Love never dies. Inspired speech will be over some day; praying in tongues will end; understanding will reach its limit. We know only a portion of the truth, and what we say about God is always incomplete. But when the Complete arrives, our incompletes will be canceled.*

*When I was an infant at my mother's breast, I gurgled and cooed like any infant. When I grew up, I left those infant ways for good.*

*We don't yet see things clearly. We're squinting in a fog, peering through a mist. But it won't be long before the weather clears and the sun shines bright! We'll see it all then, see it all as clearly as God sees us, knowing him directly just as he knows us!*

*But for right now, until that completeness, we have three things to do to lead us toward that consummation: Trust steadily in God, hope unswervingly, love extravagantly. And the best of the three is love.*

I CORINTHIANS 13:8-13

### TIMING IS THE FATHER'S BUSINESS

When that I was and a little tiny boy,
With hey-ho, the wind and the rain,
A foolish thing was but a toy,
For the rain it raineth every day.

But when I came to man's estate,
With hey-ho, the wind and the rain,
'Gainst knaves and thieves men shut their gate,
For the rain it raineth every day.

But when I came, alas, to wive,
With hey-ho, the wind and the rain,
By swaggering could I never thrive,
For the rain it raineth every day.

But when I came unto my beds,
With hey-ho, the wind and the rain,
With toss-pots still had drunken heads,
For the rain it raineth every day.

A great while ago the world began
With hey-ho, the wind and the rain,
But that's all one, our play is done,
And we'll strive to please you every day.

### TWELFTH NIGHT, EPILOGUE

### TIMING IS THE FATHER'S BUSINESS

*After his death, he presented himself alive to them in many different settings over a period of forty days. In face-to-face meetings, he talked to them about things concerning the kingdom of God. As they met and ate meals together, he told them that they were on no account to leave Jerusalem but "must wait for what the Father promised: the promise you heard from me. John baptized in water; you will be baptized in the Holy Spirit. And soon."*

*When they were together for the last time they asked, "Master, are you going to restore the kingdom to Israel now? Is this the time?"*

*He told them, "You don't get to know the time. Timing is the Father's business. What you'll get is the Holy Spirit. And when the Holy Spirit comes on you, you will be able to be my witnesses in Jerusalem, all over Judea and Samaria, even to the ends of the world."*

*These were his last words. As they watched, he was taken up and disappeared in a cloud. They stood there, staring into the empty sky. Suddenly two men appeared—in white robes! They said, "You Galileans!—why do you just stand here looking up at an empty sky? This very Jesus who was taken up from among you to heaven will come as certainly—and mysteriously—as he left."*

ACTS 1:2-11

### A GOOD MAN

When thou reviewst this, thou dost review
The very part was consecrate to Thee.
The earth can have but earth, which is his due,
My spirit is Thine, the better part of me.

SONNET 74, 5-8

### A GOOD MAN

*By now it was noon. The whole earth became dark, the darkness lasting three hours—a total blackout. The Temple curtain split right down the middle. Jesus called loudly, "Father, I place my life in your hands!" Then he breathed his last.*

*When the captain there saw what happened, he honored God: "This man was innocent! A good man, and innocent!"*

*All who had come around as spectators to watch the show, when they saw what actually happened, were overcome with grief and headed home. Those who knew Jesus well, along with the women who had followed him from Galilee, stood at a respectful distance and kept vigil.*

LUKE 23:44-49

Ron Marasco has been a Professor in the College of Communication and Fine Arts at Loyola Marymount University in Los Angeles for the last 25 years. His first book, *Notes to an Actor* was named by the American Library Association as an "Outstanding Academic Book of 2008." His second book, *About Grief: Insights, Setbacks, Grace Notes, Taboos*, written with Brian Shuff, has been translated into Spanish and Korean and published in Latin America and Asia. He has always been a working actor, appearing in an array of TV shows from *West Wing* to *Bones* to originating the role of Mr. Casper on *Freaks and Geeks*, to his recent recurring role of "Judge Grove" on *Major Crimes*, to playing the lead opposite screen-legend Kirk Douglas in the movie *Illusion*. A native of Washington Township, New Jersey, Ron has a B.A in English from Fordham University and an M.A. and Ph.D. in Theater from U.C.L.A.

## LITERARY PORTALS TO PRAYER™

Louisa May Alcott

Hans Christian Andersen

Jane Austen

Charles Dickens

Elizabeth Gaskell

Herman Melville

Enhanced-size edition available for each title.